Unit

Greater Numbers

BIG IDEAS!

- You can use place value to read, write, and describe numbers.

- You can use number and place-value patterns to solve problems.

- You can use place value or the number line to compare and order.

Songs and Games

Math Music Track 6
Count by 100s
eGames
www.eduplace.com/txmap/

Literature

Literature Big Book
- 100th Day Worries

Math Readers

Copyright © 2009 Houghton Mifflin Company.
All rights reserved.
ISBN-13: 978-0-618-95290-8
ISBN-10: 0-618-95290-X
23456789- WC - 16 15 14 13 12 11 10 09 08

Get Ready **Game**

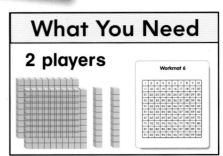
Spin a Number

How to Play

1. Spin the spinner two times. Write both numbers.

2. Find the sum. Take that many tens.

3. Regroup 10 tens for 1 hundred if you can.

4. Write the hundreds and tens. Write the number.

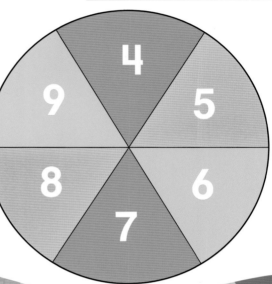

First spin	Second spin	Sum

_____ Hundreds _____ Tens _____

First spin	Second spin	Sum

_____ Hundreds _____ Tens _____

First spin	Second spin	Sum

_____ Hundreds _____ Tens _____

First spin	Second spin	Sum

_____ Hundreds _____ Tens _____

First spin	Second spin	Sum

_____ Hundreds _____ Tens _____

First spin	Second spin	Sum

_____ Hundreds _____ Tens _____

Copyright © Houghton Mifflin Company. All rights reserved.

TEKS 2.1A Use concrete models of hundreds, tens, and ones to represent a given whole number (up to 999) in various ways.

TEKS 2.1B Use place value to read, write, and describe the value of whole numbers to 999.

Education Place
Visit **eduplace.com/txmap** for eGames and Brain Teasers.

Dear Family,

My class is starting Unit 6: **Greater Numbers**. I will learn about reading, writing, ordering and comparing numbers through 999. You can help me learn these vocabulary words, and we can do the Math Activity together.

From,

_____

Vocabulary

hundred

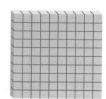

100 ones = 1 hundred
10 tens = 1 hundred

digit Any one of these ten numerals:
0, 1, 2, 3, 4, 5, 6, 7, 8, 9

39
↑↑
digits

39 has two digits

Education Place
Visit **www.eduplace.com/txmaf/** for
• More games and activities
• Math at Home in other languages

Family Math Activity

Game for 2 players: Make a set of cards with the digits 0–9. Place the cards face down. Each player takes 3 cards and makes a 3-digit number. Each players says their number. The player with the greater number wins the round. Replace and shuffle the cards. The winner is the player that wins two out of three rounds.

0 1 2 3 4 5 6 7 8 9

Literature

These books link to the math in this unit. Look for them at the library.
• **A Million Fish...More or Less** by Patricia C. McKissack (*Dragonfly Books*, 1996)
• **One Grain of Rice** by Demi
• **Earth Day — Hooray!** by Stuart J. Murphy

Matemáticas en casa

Estimada familia:

Mi clase está comenzando la Unidad 6, **Números más grandes**. Voy a aprender a leer, escribir, ordenar y comparar números hasta el 999. Me pueden ayudar a aprender estas palabras de vocabulario y podemos hacer juntos la Actividad de matemáticas para la familia.

De:

_____

Vocabulario

centena

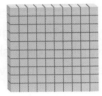

100 unidades = 1 centena
10 decenas = 1 centena

dígito Cualquiera de estos diez números:
0, 1, 2, 3, 4, 5, 6, 7, 8, 9

39
↑↑
dígitos

39 tiene dos dígitos

 Education Place
Visite **www.eduplace.com/txmaf/** para
• Más juegos y actividades
• Matemáticas en casa, en otros idiomas

Actividad de matemáticas para la familia

Juego para 2 jugadores: Haga un conjunto de tarjetas con los dígitos 0 al 9. Coloque las tarjetas boca abajo. Cada jugador toma 3 tarjetas y forma un número de 3 dígitos. Cada jugador dice su número. El jugador que tenga el número más grande gana la ronda. Devuelva y baraje las tarjetas. El ganador es el jugador que gane dos de tres rondas.

Literatura

Estos libros hablan sobre las matemáticas de esta unidad. Podemos buscarlos en la biblioteca.

• **Los 500 sombreros de Bartolomé Cubbins**
  por Dr. Seuss
  (*Lectorum publications*)

• **¡Todos ganan!**

"Finding Ten"

written by Mike Mason

This Take-Home Book belongs to

Reading and Writing Math

This take-home book will help you review tens and ones.

When Keri got home she got busy! Look at the great things she made for the sale!

TAKS Objective 1
TEKS 2.1A

Keri will make things for a craft fair.
Keri has a list of things she needs to
get for her crafts.
Can you read her list?

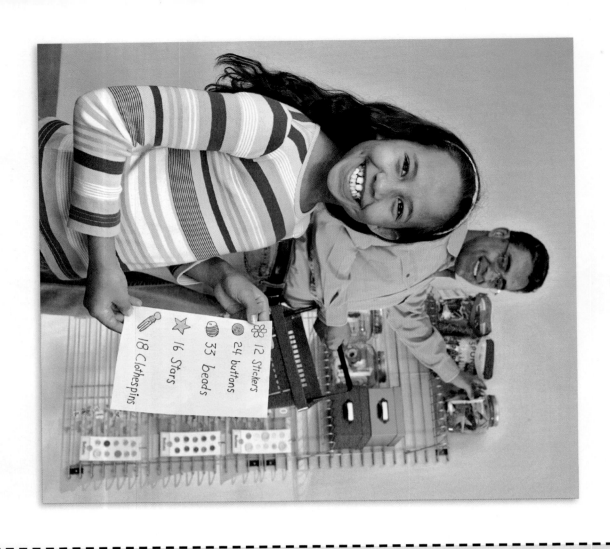

Keri needs 18 clothespins.
Which clothespins will she buy?
Circle them.

Copyright © Houghton Mifflin Company. All rights reserved.

Keri needs 12 stickers for her project.
The stickers are sold in sets of ten or one
at a time.
Circle the stickers you think Keri will buy.

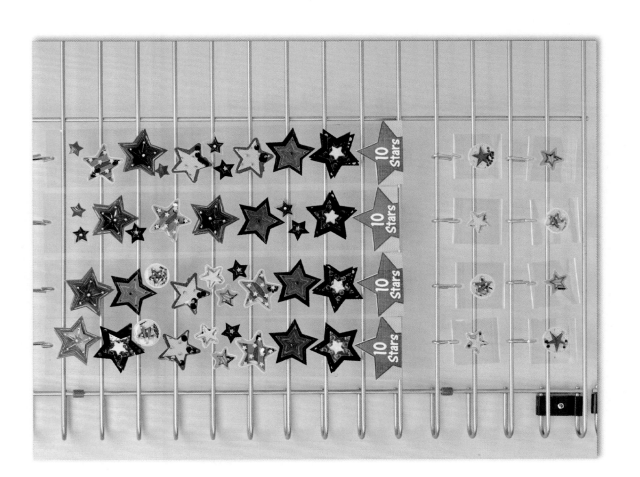

Keri needs 16 stars. Stars are sold in
sets of ten, or as single stars.
Circle the stars you think Keri will buy.

Keri needs 24 buttons. The buttons are sold in sets of ten or as single buttons. Circle the buttons you think Keri will buy.

Next, Keri needs 33 beads. Beads are sold in sets of ten, or as single beads. Circle the beads you think Keri will buy.

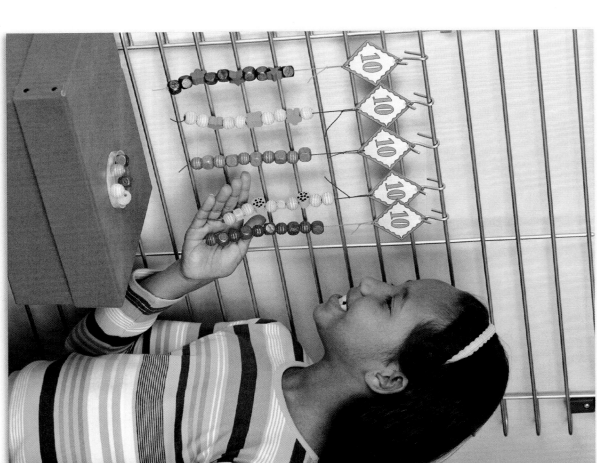

Copyright © Houghton Mifflin Company. All rights reserved.

5

Greater Numbers

TAKS Vocabulary

Here are some vocabulary words you will learn in the chapter.

hundreds Ten groups of ten is the same as one hundred.

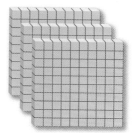

3 hundreds
300

digit Any of the numbers
0, 1, 2, 3, 4, 5, 6, 7, 8, 9

461
↑↑↑

4, 6, and 1 are the 3 digits in 461.

See English-Spanish glossary pages 537–548.

TAKS Objective 6
TEKS 2.13B Relate informal language to mathematical language and symbols.

Education Place
Visit **www.eduplace.com/txmap/** for the eGlossary and vocabulary eGames. two hundred seventy-one **271**

Name _____

1. Show the number **83** as tens and ones.

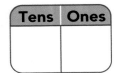

2. Show the number **58** as tens and ones.

Tens	Ones

3. Which number has more tens, **64** or **27**?
   How do you know?

   _____ has more tens because

   _____

4. Circle the value of the **7** in the number **27**.

   7 tens   **7** ones

5. Circle the value of the **3** in the number **39**.

   3 tens   **3** ones

Use this page to review important skills needed for this chapter.

272

Copyright © Houghton Mifflin Company. All rights reserved.

Name _____

Hundreds, Tens, and Ones

★ Learn

There are 134 apartments in Myra's building. Show 134 two other ways.

You can show a number with blocks or as **hundreds,** tens, and ones. You can use numbers.

Hands On 👋

TEKS Objective
Use models to count by hundreds, tens, and ones; write numbers through 999.

TAKS Vocabulary
hundreds

Workmat 6		
hundreds	tens	ones
[flat block]	[3 rods]	[4 units]

Hundreds	Tens	Ones
1	3	4

_134_

one hundred thirty-four

★ Guided Practice

Work together. Write the amount as hundreds, tens, and ones and with numbers.

Think!
I write the number of hundreds, tens, and ones.

1. Show 1 [flat], 4 [rods], and 7 [units].

Hundreds	Tens	Ones
1	4	7

_147_

2. Show 1 [flat], 5 [rods], and 2 [units].

Hundreds	Tens	Ones

_____

3. Show 1 [flat] and 2 [rods].

Hundreds	Tens	Ones

_____

4. Show 1 [flat] and 6 [units].

Hundreds	Tens	Ones

_____

5. **(123)** **Math Talk** Explain why the 1 does not have the same value in the numbers 361 and 163.

 **TAKS Objective 1**
TEKS 2.1A Use concrete models of hundreds, tens, and ones to represent a given whole number (up to 999) in various ways.

TEKS 2.1B Use place value to read, write, and describe the value of whole numbers to 999.

two hundred seventy-three **273**

Work together.
Use Workmat 6 with 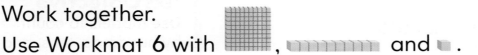, and .

Remember!
= 100.

	Show this many.	Write how many hundreds, tens, and ones.	Write the number.
6.		Hundreds | Tens | Ones 2 | 4 | 2	242
7.		Hundreds | Tens | Ones	_____
8.		Hundreds | Tens | Ones	_____
9.		Hundreds | Tens | Ones	_____

10. In the space at the right,
    draw a picture to show 627.

Problem Solving: Reasoning

Circle the best answer.

11. I go to school about _____ days each year.   2   20   200

12. My class has about _____ children.   2   20   200

At Home Have your child collect 100 objects, such as buttons or beans, and count them in groups of 10.

En casa Pida a su niño que reúna 100 objetos, como botones o frijoles, y que los cuente en grupos de 10.

Copyright © Houghton Mifflin Company. All rights reserved.

Name _____

Chapter 14 Lesson 2

Trade Ones and Tens Game

★ **Learn**

Work with a partner.
You will need Workmat 3, 1 number
cube (1–6), ⬚⬚⬚⬚⬚, and ▪.

To Play:
Roll the cube. Take the number of ▪
as shown on the cube. When you can,
trade 10 ▪ for 1 ⬚⬚⬚⬚⬚.
The first player to reach 10 ⬚⬚⬚⬚⬚,
or 100, is the winner.

★ **Guided Practice**

Record on the score sheet.

Number on Cube	Can I Make a Trade?	Tens	Ones

1. **123** **Math Talk** On your turn, how will you know if
you can make a trade?

TAKS Objective 1
TEKS 2.1A Use concrete models of hundreds,
tens, and ones to represent a given whole number
(up to 999) in various ways.

TEKS 2.1B Use place value to read, write, and
describe the value of whole numbers to 999.

two hundred seventy-five **275**

Complete the puzzle.

Across

1. 6 hundreds 7 tens 3 ones

3.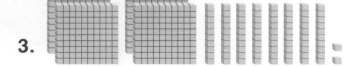

5. three hundred forty-nine

6. 3 hundreds 9 tens 3 ones

8.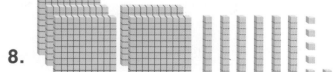

11. one hundred eight

14. 34 tens

15. 2 hundreds 3 tens 6 ones

16.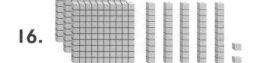

Down

1. 6 hundreds 5 tens 3 ones

2. three hundred thirty-three

3.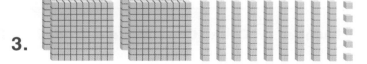

4. 2 hundreds 2 tens 6 ones

7.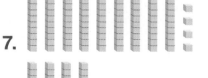

9.

10. 4 hundreds 3 tens 5 ones

11. 1 hundred 3 ones

12. 8 hundreds 2 tens 2 ones

13. 4 hundreds 6 tens 4 ones

Copyright © Houghton Mifflin Company. All rights reserved.

At Home Ask your child how to play the game on page 275. What is *making a trade?*

En casa Pida a su niño que explique cómo jugar el juego de la página 275. ¿Qué es *reagrupar?*

Chapter 14 Lesson 3

Place Value to 999

TEKS **Objective**
Identify place value to 999.

TAKS **Vocabulary**
digit

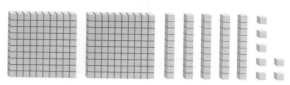 **Learn**

To find the value of a **digit,** find the value of its place. Find the value of the digits in 257.

Hundreds	Tens	Ones
2	5	7

200 + 50 + 7

257

The 2 is in the hundreds place. Its value is 200.

The 5 is in the tens place. Its value is 50.

The 7 is in the ones place. Its value is 7.

Reunion Tower in Dallas

Guided Practice

Write the number.

1. $900 + 60 + 1 =$ _____

2. $600 + 50 + 2 =$ _____

Think!
I write 9 in the hundreds place, 6 in the tens place, and 1 in the ones place.

3. $800 + 50 + 3 =$ _____

4. $300 + 4 =$ _____

5. $8 + 60 + 300 =$ _____

6. $7 + 100 =$ _____

Circle the value of the red digit.

7.
849

800   80   8

8.
962

600   60   6

9.
294

400   40   4

10. **123** **Math Talk** What does the digit 0 in 704 mean?

 TAKS Objective 1
TEKS 2.1B Use place value to read, write, and describe the value of whole numbers to 999.

Write the number.

Remember!
To find the value of a digit, find the value of its place.

11. $1 + 20 + 300 =$ _321_

12. $4 + 80 + 200 =$ _____

13. $6 + 800 =$ _____

14. $7 + 60 =$ _____

15. $3 + 10 + 400 =$ _____

16. $600 + 30 + 2 =$ _____

17. $7 + 50 + 800 =$ _____

Circle the value of the red digit.

18. | 492 | 400   40   4

19. | 781 | 800   80   8

20. | 352 | 300   30   3

21. | 527 | 200   20   2

22. | 637 | 700   70   7

23. | 576 | 500   50   5

24. Write a 3-digit number with a 5 in the tens place. _____

Problem Solving: Number Sense

Solve.

25. Mavis has 2 tens rods, 2 ones blocks and 4 hundreds flats. What number can she show?

_____

26. Nam shows 657 using quick pictures. Show 657 another way.

_____

Copyright © Houghton Mifflin Company. All rights reserved.

At Home Write a three-digit number, such as 465 or 891. Have your child name the value of the digit in the tens place.

En casa Escriba un número de tres dígitos, como 465 u 891. Pida a su niño que diga el valor del dígito en la posición de las decenas.

Find a Pattern

Problem Solving
Strategy

TEKS Objective
Solve problems using a pattern.

Sometimes you can find a pattern to help solve a problem.

Toby's family is planning a block party. They asked **5** neighbors to bring paper plates.

Understand

Circle what you need to find out.

How many paper plates did each neighbor bring?

How many paper plates did all 5 neighbors bring?

Plan

Make a table and look for a pattern. What information will be in your table?

_____ neighbors

_____ paper plates from each neighbor

Solve

Make a table.

Neighbors	1	2	3	4	
Paper plates	100	200	300		

The neighbors brought _____ paper plates in all.

Look Back

How does knowing about hundreds help you find the pattern?

 TAKS Objectives 2 and 6
TEKS 2.6A Generate a list of paired numbers based on a real-life situation such as number of triangles related to number of wheels.

Also **TEKS 2.6C, TEKS 2.12C**

1. 4 of Toby's neighbors brought balloons.
   Each person brought 8 balloons.
   How many balloons were brought in all?

   Make a table.

   How many people brought balloons? _____

   How many balloons did each person bring? _____

People	1			
Balloons	8			

   _____ balloons

2. (123) **Math Talk** How did you find the number
   of balloons 2 people brought?

Solve. Complete the table and look for a pattern.

3. Some people are racing on the grass.
   Each team has 6 people. If 30 people are racing,
   how many teams are there?

Teams	1				
People	6				

   _____ teams

4. A few children caught fireflies. They caught 10 fireflies
   in each jar. How many fireflies are in 4 jars?

Jars	1			
Fireflies	10			

   _____ fireflies

Copyright © Houghton Mifflin Company. All rights reserved.

At Home Have your child explain
how he or she completed the tables to
help solve the problems.

En casa Pida a su niño que explique cómo
completó las tablas como ayuda para resolver
los problemas.

Social Studies

Texas Field Trip
Community Fire Department

You can visit your local fire department to learn about fire safety and prevention. You can see the equipment used by the firefighters. You can explore the fire engines and other safety vehicles.

A fire station in Dallas, Texas

Solve. Show your work.

1. A pumper truck holds **750** gallons of water. Write that amount as hundreds, tens, and ones.

   pumper truck

   750 = _____ + _____ + _____

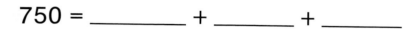

2. **25** children visited the fire station on Monday. **33** children visited on Tuesday. How many more were there on Tuesday than on Monday?

   firefighter

   _____ children

3. A firefighter gave away **52** fire prevention stickers and **43** fire safety books. How many stickers and books were given away in all?

   safety book

   _____ stickers and books

TAKS Objective 1
TEKS 2.1B Use place value to read, write, and describe the value of whole numbers to 999.
TEKS 2.3C Select addition or subtraction to solve problems using two-digit numbers, whether or not regrouping is necessary.
Social Studies TEKS 13C

Create and Solve

Gina's friends worked in the park on Saturday.

Gina made up this problem. Solve her problem.

Work Done on Saturday
Picked up 368 cans.
Picked up 100 fewer
bottles than cans.
Planted 203 marigolds.
Planted some daisies.

1. The friends planted 100 more daisies than marigolds. How many daisies did they plant?

   _____ + _____ = _____

2. Write your own problem about the work in the park. Use 3-digit numbers. Solve your problem.

   _____

   _____

   _____

   _____

   _____

   _____ $\bigcirc$ _____ = _____

Name _____

Patterns and Place Value

TEKS Objective
Observe and use patterns in place value.

★ Learn

Patterns help you compare and order numbers.
Look at the chart.
Look at the pattern as the digits change.
Which digit changes? How does the number change?

Hundreds	Tens	Ones
1	3	4
1	3	5
1	3	6

The ones digit changes.
The numbers increase by 1.

Hundreds	Tens	Ones
1	3	4
1	4	4
1	5	4

The tens digit changes.
The numbers increase by ____.

Hundreds	Tens	Ones
1	3	4
2	3	4
3	3	4

_____
_____
_____

★ Guided Practice

Start with 527.

1. Increase by 10.

Hundreds	Tens	Ones
5	2	7
5	3	7
5	4	7

2. Increase by 100.

Hundreds	Tens	Ones

3. (123) **Math Talk** In the number 601, what value does the 0 have?

TAKS Objective 2
TEKS 2.5B Use patterns in place value to compare and order whole numbers through 999.

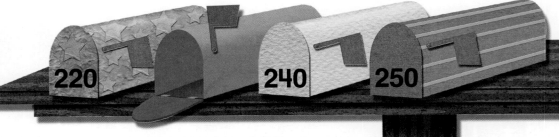

★ Practice

Start with 343.

4. Increase by 10.

Hundreds	Tens	Ones
3	4	3

5. Increase by 100.

Hundreds	Tens	Ones

Make a pattern. Increase by 10.

6. 327, _____, _____, _____

7. 748, _____, _____, _____

8. 516, _____, _____, _____

9. 432, _____, _____, _____

Make a pattern. Increase by 100.

10. 625, _____, _____, _____

11. 153, _____, _____, _____

12. 333, _____, _____, _____

13. 202, _____, _____, _____

14. Make a pattern increasing by 10.

568, _____, _____, _____, _____, _____

Problem Solving: Reasoning

Solve.

Draw or write to explain.

15. Will is thinking of a number. It has a 1 in the tens digit, a 9 in the ones digit, and a 6 in the hundreds digit. What is the number?

_____

Copyright © Houghton Mifflin Company. All rights reserved.

□□|||||||°°°°

At Home Write a three-digit number such as 452 and ask your child how many hundreds, tens, and ones it has.

En casa Escriba un número de tres dígitos como 452 y pregunte a su niño cuántas centenas, decenas y unidades tiene.

Name _____

Texas Star Hibiscus

The Texas Star Hibiscus is a common flower in Texas. It likes water and warm, sunny days.

Solve. Draw or write to explain.

1. Mrs. Rodriguez has 127 hibiscus seeds to start new plants. She wants 100 more. How many will she have altogether?

   _____ seeds

2. The number of hibiscus plants in the park has a **2** in the ones digit, a **1** in the hundreds digit, and a **6** in the tens digit. How many hibiscus plants are in the park?

   _____ hibiscus

3. Mrs. Rodriguez puts 10 plants in each row. How many plants will she have if she has 7 rows?

Rows	1	2	3	4	5	6	7
Plants	___	___	___	___	___	___	___

_____ plants

TAKS Objectives 1 and 2
TEKS 2.1B Use place value to read, write, and describe the value of whole numbers to 999.

TEKS 2.5B Use patterns in place value to compare and order whole numbers through 999. Also **TEKS 2.6B**
TEKS Science 9A

Greater Number Patterns

Use your calculator.
Make a + 50 pattern.

Start by putting the number in your calculator.
Then:

- Press **+** **5** **0**

- Press **=**

- Continue to press **=** to find the missing numbers.
  328, 378, _____, _____, _____

---

1. Make a pattern with **−** 75.

   403, 328, _____, _____, _____

2. Make a pattern with **+** 85.

   403, 488, _____, _____, _____

3. Make a pattern with **−** 35.

   403, 368, _____, _____, _____

425, 450
475, 500
525

TAKS Objective 6
TEKS 2.12D Use tools such as real objects, manipulatives, and technology to solve problems.

Education Place
Visit www.eduplace.com/txmap/
for more activities.

Houghton Mifflin Company. All rights reserved.

Name _____

Concepts and Skills

Count hundreds, tens, and ones.
Write the number. TEKS 2.1A, 2.1B

1. 3 [   ], 5 [   ], and 2

Hundreds	Tens	Ones

_____

2. 2 [   ], 6 [   ], and 4

Hundreds	Tens	Ones

_____

Write the missing numbers.

3. Count by 100.

   100 200 _____ 400 500 _____ 700 _____ 900

---

4. Count by 50.

   50 100 150 _____ 250 300 _____ _____ 450

Problem Solving

Complete the table. Solve. TEKS 2.6B

Groups	1	2	3	4	5	6
Children	5	___	___	___	___	___

5. Coach has arranged 6 groups of children to
   practice soccer. There are 5 children in each
   group. How many children are practicing?

   _____ children

TAKS Prep and Spiral Review

Choose the answer for Problems 1-3.

1. 36 cars are parked in front of the library. Some cars are parked at the side. There are 58 cars in all. How many are parked at the side?

22 ○   14 ○   56 ○   68 ○

TEKS 2.3C (page 183)

2. The graph shows the number of boxes of cookies each class sold. How many more boxes of cookies were sold by Mrs. Brown's class than Mr. Todd's class?

Boxes of Cookies Sold

Mrs. Brown	🍪 🍪 🍪 🍪 🍪
Mr. Todd	🍪 🍪 🍪
Mrs. Stevens	🍪 🍪 🍪 🍪

Key: Each 🍪 = 5 boxes

5 boxes ○   2 boxes ○   10 boxes ○   1 box ○

TEKS 2.11B (page 121)

3. The library has 55 books on animals. 14 of them are checked out. How many animal books are still in the library?

31 ○   41 ○   49 ○   69 ○

TEKS 2.3C (page 249)

Education Place
Visit www.eduplace.com/txmap/ for Test-Taking Tips and Extra Practice.

Spiral Review

TAKS Vocabulary

Here are some vocabulary words you will use in this chapter.

place value The value of the place where a digit is

3 hundreds = 300   2 tens = 20   5 ones = 5

before, after, between Words used to order numbers

145 146 147 148 149 150 151 152 153 154 155 156 157 158 159 160

147 is before 148   152 is between   160 is after 159
151 and 153

greater than, less than, equal to Words used to compare numbers

214 > 125
214 is greater than 125

226 < 231
226 is less than 231

226 = 226
226 is equal to 226

See English-Spanish glossary pages 537–548.

TAKS Objective 6
TEKS 2.13B Relate informal language to mathematical language and symbols.

Education Place
Visit **www.eduplace.com/txmap/** for the eGlossary and vocabulary eGames.

Name _____

✓ Check What You Know

Use the tickets to solve.

1. Which concert ticket number comes before 23?

   ticket number _____

2. Which concert ticket number comes between 86 and 49?

   ticket number _____

3. What is the order of the ticket numbers from least to greatest?

   _____, _____, _____, _____, _____

4. Which ticket numbers are greater than 18 but less than 57?

   _____ and _____

5. Create a new ticket number that is less than 23 but greater than 18.

   _____

Use this page to review important skills needed for this chapter.

290

Copyright © Houghton Mifflin Company. All rights reserved.

Name _____

Before, After, Between

★ Explore

Hands On

TEKS Objective
Order three-digit numbers.

TAKS Vocabulary
before
after
between

Mario and Sue have several tickets to the school concert. The tickets are blue.

A number line can help you find a number that is just before, just after, or between other numbers.

Cut out the tickets on the side of this page. Use the number line to help put the tickets in order.

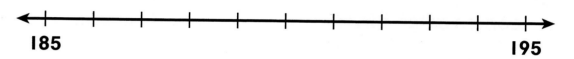

185   195

1. What ticket number comes **before** 192? _____

2. What ticket number comes **after** 189? _____

3. What ticket number comes before 194? _____

4. What ticket number comes **between** 189 and 191? _____

5. (123) **Math Talk** Is there a ticket number between 188 and 189? Explain.

191

189

188

194

193

190

192

TAKS Objective 3
TEKS 2.8 Use whole numbers to locate and name points on a number line.

two hundred ninety-one **291**

Use the pink tickets.
Put the tickets in order.
You can use the number line.

Remember!
You can also count to find a number.

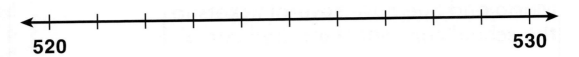

520   530

527

523

526

522

528

525

524 ✓

6. What ticket number comes before 526? _____

7. What ticket number comes between 525 and 527? _____

8. What ticket number comes after 522? _____

9. You have ticket number 531. What ticket number comes next? _____

What ticket number comes before? _____

Problem Solving: Number Sense

10. Jason has 4 tickets. Write the numbers in order on the number line.

629 631 628 630

_____ _____ _____ _____

11. What number should come next? _____

12. What number should come just before these tickets? _____

Copyright © Houghton Mifflin Company. All rights reserved.

At Home Write a three-digit number. Ask your child to write the numbers that come just before and just after it.

En casa Escriba un número de tres dígitos. Pida a su niño que escriba los números que vienen justo antes y justo después del número.

Compare Three-Digit Numbers

 **Learn**

TEKS Objective
Use place value to compare three-digit numbers.

TAKS Vocabulary
place value
least
greatest

Look at the chart. What pattern do you
see in the hundreds, tens, and ones?

Hundreds	Tens	Ones
2	5	5
2	6	5
2	7	5
2	8	5

Use **place value** to compare numbers.
You can find which number is the **least**
and which number is the **greatest.**

Compare 255 and 265.

First compare hundreds. If the hundreds
are the same, compare the tens.

255 is less than 265
255 < 265

Guided Practice

Think!
Compare the hundreds,
then the tens, then
the ones.

Use patterns in the place-value chart.
Compare the numbers. Write >, <, or = in the ◯.

1. 265 ◯ 275

2. 265 ◯ 285

3. 275 ◯ 255

4. 305 ◯ 295

5. 315 ◯ 315

6. 265 ◯ 305

7. **(123)** **Math Talk** How does knowing about place
value help you compare numbers?

TAKS Objectives 1 and 2
TEKS 2.5B Use patterns in place value to order
whole numbers through 999.

TEKS 2.1C Use place value to compare and order
whole numbers to 999 and record the comparisons
using numbers and symbols (<, =, >).

Remember!
Compare the hundreds first, then the tens, then the ones.

Use patterns in the place-value chart. Compare the numbers. Write >, <, or = in the ◯.

Hundreds	Tens	Ones
1	0	5
1	1	0
1	1	5
1	2	0
1	2	5

8. 105 ◯ 115

9. 115 ◯ 125

10. 120 ◯ 105

11. 125 ◯ 120

12. 105 ◯ 105

13. 115 ◯ 120

Hundreds	Tens	Ones
6	8	1
7	8	2
8	8	3
9	8	4

14. 782 ◯ 681

15. 681 ◯ 984

16. 883 ◯ 984

17. 782 ◯ 782

18. 883 ◯ 681

19. 984 ◯ 784

20. **123** **Math Talk** For Exercises 14–19, did you use the pattern in the hundreds, tens, or ones place to compare the numbers? Tell why.

Problem Solving: Reasoning

21. Joe has seat number 632 at the concert. Ling has seat number 487. Carlos has seat number 556. Whose seat number has the greatest number? Tell how you know.

_____

Copyright © Houghton Mifflin Company. All rights reserved.

🏠 **At Home** Write 2 three-digit numbers. Ask your child which number is greater.

En casa Escriba 2 números de tres dígitos. Pregunte a su niño qué número es mayor.

Problem Solving: Reasoning

Shakim and his cousin David are
going to a concert in Dallas.

Draw or write to explain.

22. Shakim travels 247 miles
to the concert. David travels
277 miles to the concert.
Who travels farther?

_____

23. Shakim cannot remember if his
ticket number is **804** or **704**.
David knows his ticket number is
greater than **800**. Which number
is Shakim's ticket if he is sitting
next to David?

_____

24. Shakim and David go to
Dallas again in **352** days.
Is that more or less than
one year?

Think!
A year has 365 days.

_____

Use each digit.
Write a **3**-digit number to make a true sentence.

Ticket 2 **Ticket 4** **Ticket 6**

1. ____ ____ ____ > 526

2. ____ ____ ____ < 526

3. ____ ____ ____ < 256

4. ____ ____ ____ > 624

Real World Data

Elm Fork Nature Preserve

Elm Fork Nature Preserve is open 365 days a year. Visitors can camp and hike there.

1. Which month had the most visitors?

   _____

2. Which month had the least visitors?

   _____

Month	Number of Visitors
May	383
June	595
July	437

Copyright © Houghton Mifflin Company. All rights reserved.

TAKS Objective 1
TEKS 2.1 B Use place value to read, write, and describe the value of whole numbers to 999.
Also **TEKS 2.1C**

Education Place
Visit **www.eduplace.com/txmap/** for Brain Teasers.

Order Three-Digit Numbers

TEKS Objective
Use place value to order three-digit numbers.

★ Learn

Ordering numbers is like comparing pairs of numbers from a list. You can use patterns in place value to help.

| 212 | 159 | 215 |

Step 1 Compare the hundreds. Write the number with the fewest hundreds.

159 _____ _____ _____

Hundreds	Tens	Ones
2	1	2

Step 2 Compare the tens.

Hundreds	Tens	Ones
1	5	9

Step 3 Compare the ones. 2 < 5. Write the numbers in order.

159 _____ _____ _____

Hundreds	Tens	Ones
2	1	5

Think!
640 and 635 both have 6 hundreds, so I compare the tens.

★ Guided Practice

Write the numbers in order from least to greatest.

1. 640   540   630   _____   _____   _____

2. 781   780   308   _____   _____   _____

Write the numbers in order from greatest to least.

3. 125   135   435   _____   _____   _____

4. 343   333   434   _____   _____   _____

5. **(123) Math Talk** How does knowing about place value help you order numbers?

TAKS Objectives 1 and 2
TEKS 2.5B Use patterns in place value to order whole numbers through 999.

TEKS 2.1C Use place value to compare and order whole numbers to 999 and record the comparisons using numbers and symbols (<, =, >).

Remember!
Use place value to
order numbers.

Write the numbers in order
from least to greatest.

Make a place value chart to help.
Look for patterns.

6. 199   154   291   192   _154_   _192_   _199_   _291_

7. 430   434   426   438   _____   _____   _____   _____

8. 795   800   790   805   _____   _____   _____   _____

Write the numbers in order from greatest to least.

9. 175   180   165   170   _____   _____   _____   _____

10. 922   924   920   918   _____   _____   _____   _____

11. 723   823   623   923   _____   _____   _____   _____

Problem Solving: Reasoning

Solve.

Draw or write to explain.

12. Which number is out of order if Paul
is ordering numbers from least to
greatest? How do you know?

715   775   735   762

_____ is out of order.

Copyright © Houghton Mifflin Company. All rights reserved.

At Home Write 3 three-digit numbers.
Have your child put the numbers in
order from greatest to least.

En casa Escriba 3 números de tres dígitos.
Pida a su niño que ponga los números en
orden de mayor a menor.

Name _____

Chapter 15 Lesson 4

Different Ways to Show Numbers

TEKS Objective
Use words, models, and expanded form to show numbers in different ways.

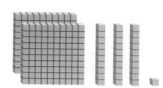 **Learn**

Here are three ways to show 231.

Use models.

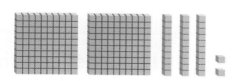

Write the number of hundreds, tens, and ones.

2 hundreds 3 tens 1 one

Show the number with addition.

200 + 30 + 1

Think!
There is a zero in the tens place because there are no tens.

Guided Practice

Circle another way to show the number.

1.

302

3 hundreds 0 tens
2 ones

2.

415

400 + 10 + 5

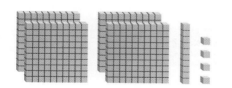

3. 150

5 hundreds 1 ten 3 ones

100 + 50

Draw or write to show the number another way.

4.

217

5.

326

6. **Math Talk** How could you show 555 with the least number of hundreds, tens, and ones blocks?

TAKS Objective 1
TEKS 2.1A Use concrete models of hundreds, tens, and ones to represent a given whole number (up to 999) in various ways.

Remember!
Look for the same number of hundreds, tens, and ones.

Circle another way to show the number.

7.

| 442 |

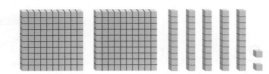

$\left(\!\overline{400 + 40 + 2}\!\right)$

8.

| 205 |

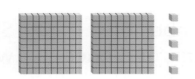

$200 + 10 + 5$

9.

| 640 |

$600 + 40$ 6 hundreds 0 tens 4 ones

10.

| 754 |

$700 + 50 + 4$ 7 hundreds 4 tens 5 ones

11. Draw or write to show the number another way.

| 485 |

12. Cross out the one that does not belong.

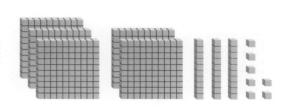

537   500 + 70 + 3

5 hundreds 3 tens 7 ones

Problem Solving: Number Sense

13. Luis counts pages in his story books.
2 books have 100 pages each.
3 books have 10 pages each.
One book has 6 pages. How many pages are there altogether?

_____ pages

Copyright © Houghton Mifflin Company. All rights reserved.

At Home Choose a 3-digit number. Ask your child how many hundreds, tens, and ones there are.

En casa Elija un número de 3 dígitos. Pregunte a su niño cuántas centenas, decenas y unidades tiene.

Name _____

Use a Model

TEKS Objective
Use a model to solve problems.

★ **Learn**

You can use a model to solve a problem.

The school bought new instruments. They spent 315 dollars for violins. The drums cost 210 dollars. The flutes cost 310 dollars. On which instrument did they spend the most?

Understand
Circle what you need to find out.

How much money they spent in all.

The instrument they spent the most money for.

Plan
Use a place value chart to model the problem.

	Hundreds	Tens	Ones
Violins			
Drums			
Flutes			

Think!
Look for patterns.

Solve
Compare hundreds, then compare tens, then ones.

- 210 is less than _____ and _____.
- 310 and 315 have the same number of _____.
- 315 ◯ 310.

On which instrument did they spend the most money? _____

Look Back
How did the model help you solve the problem?

TAKS Objective 2 and 6
TEKS 2.5B Use patterns in place value to compare and order whole numbers through 999.

TEKS 2.12B Solve problems with guidance that incorporates the processes of understanding the problem, making a plan, carrying out the plan, and evaluating the solution for reasonableness.

1. Tickets are on sale for the school concert.
   302 tickets are sold on Tuesday.
   342 tickets are sold on Wednesday.
   On Thursday, 242 tickets are sold.
   What is the order of the number of
   tickets sold from greatest to least?

   Use a place value model to solve the
   problem.

	Hundreds	Tens	Ones
Tuesday			
Wednesday			
Thursday			

_____   _____   _____

2. (123) **Math Talk** Look at the completed chart in
   Problem 1. Describe any patterns you see.

Solve. Use the place value model.

3. 130 children play in the morning.
   103 play in the afternoon.
   213 play in the evening.
   Do more children play in the
   morning or the evening?

	Hundreds	Tens	Ones
Morning			
Evening			

_____

Copyright © Houghton Mifflin Company. All rights reserved.

At Home Have your child explain how he or she completed the place value charts to help solve the problems.

En casa Pida a su niño que explique cómo completó las tablas de valor de posición como ayuda para resolver los problemas.

Texas Field Trip
Morton H. Meyerson Symphony Center

At the Morton H. Meyerson Symphony Center, you can hear the Dallas Symphony Orchestra perform classical and popular music.

Social Studies

Morton H. Meyerson Symphony Center

Solve. Show your work.

1. 120 people sat on the right side.
   500 people sat in the center.
   165 people sat on the left side.
   Order the number of people from least to greatest.

   _____   _____   _____

theater

2. There are 20 first violins and 12 second violins. How many more first violins than second violins are there?

   _____ more first violins

violin

3. There are 55 trumpets and 26 flutes in a marching band. How many trumpets and flutes are there together?

   _____ trumpets and flutes

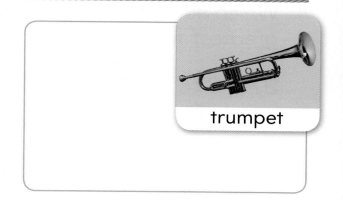
trumpet

TAKS Objective 1
TEKS 2.1.C Use place value to compare and order whole numbers to 999 and record the comparisons using numbers and symbols (<, =, >).

TEKS 2.3C Select addition or subtraction to solve problems using two-digit numbers, whether or not regrouping is necessary.
Social Studies TEKS 15A

three hundred three 303

TAKS Problem Solving
Listening Skills

Read along as your teacher reads aloud.
Choose the correct answer.

Select a Strategy
Act It Out
Draw a Picture

1. There are 113 children in the first row.
   Which does not show 113?

    100 + 13   one hundred thirteen

   ○   ○   ○   ○

TEKS 2.1B

2. 674 went to a concert.
   What number comes just before?

   672   673   675   676
    ○   ○   ○   ○

TEKS 2.1C

3. There are 322 children in Madison School,
   478 at Lincoln School, and 490 at Washington
   School. What is the greatest number
   of students in one school?

   322   478   490   522
    ○   ○   ○   ○

TEKS 2.1C

4. Which numbers are not listed in order from
   greatest to least?

   379, 376, 377   421, 392, 391
        ○   ○

   526, 520, 519   923, 329, 293
        ○   ○

TEKS 2.1C

Copyright © Houghton Mifflin Company. All rights reserved.

 **Education Place**
Visit www.eduplace.com/txmap/ for
Test-Taking Tips and more TAKS Practice.

Name _____

Map of Texas

Texas is the second largest state in the United States. The capital of Texas is Austin. The map shows the distances between Austin and some other cities in Texas.

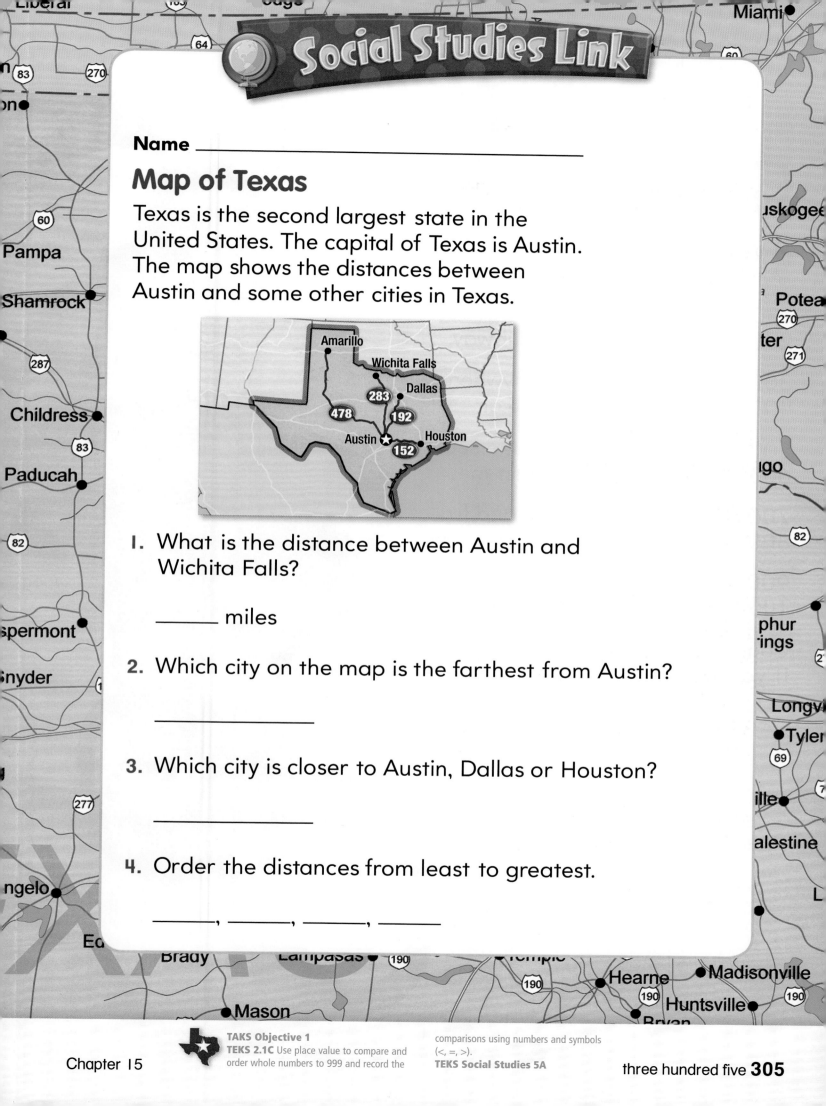

1. What is the distance between Austin and Wichita Falls?

   _____ miles

2. Which city on the map is the farthest from Austin?

   _____

3. Which city is closer to Austin, Dallas or Houston?

   _____

4. Order the distances from least to greatest.

   _____, _____, _____, _____

TAKS Objective 1
TEKS 2.1C Use place value to compare and order whole numbers to 999 and record the comparisons using numbers and symbols $(<, =, >)$.
TEKS Social Studies 5A

Math Music

Count By 100s

Math Music, Track 6
Tune: "Down in the Valley"

100 children walk quickly each day.
200 children will ride the subway.

300 children ride cars everywhere.
400 children ride jets in the air.

500 children ride boats in the sea.
600 children ride buses past me.

700 children ride trains to and fro.
800 children ride horses, you know.

900 children ride bikes just like you.
1000 children ride tricycles, too.

Count by 100s. Can you do it now?
If you can do it, then please take a bow!

Copyright © Houghton Mifflin Company. All rights reserved.

TAKS Objective 2
TEKS 2.5A Find patterns in numbers such as in a 100s chart.

Name _____

Concepts and Skills

Use the number line. Write the number. TEKS 2.1C, TEKS 2.8

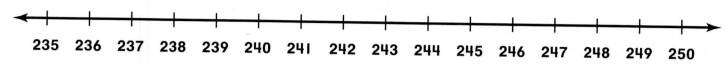

235 236 237 238 239 240 241 242 243 244 245 246 247 248 249 250

	Before	**Between**	**After**
1.	_____, 240	241, _____, 243	244, _____
2.	_____, 244	245, _____, 247	248, _____
3.	_____, 250	235, _____, 237	239, _____

Compare the numbers. Write >, <, or = in the ( ). TEKS 2.1C

4. 327 ( ) 372   5. 342 ( ) 342   6. 429 ( ) 294

Write the numbers in order from least to greatest. TEKS 2.1B, 2.1C

7. 253   235   215   325   _____ _____ _____ _____

8. 502   620   525   615   _____ _____ _____ _____

9. 452   721   297   503   _____ _____ _____ _____

Problem Solving TEKS 2.1A, 2.13B

Solve.

10. Myra's family drove 326 miles to her uncle's home.
    Show the number of miles two different ways.

    _____

TAKS Prep and Spiral Review

Choose the answer for Problems 1–4.

1. Ana sold 18 tickets on Friday and 31 tickets on Saturday. How many more tickets did she sell on Saturday than on Friday?

49	27	13	23
○	○	○	○

TEKS 2.3C (page 239)

2. There are 35 children in the band. There are 17 boys. How many girls are in the band?

53	18	22	28
○	○	○	○

TEKS 2.3C (page 239)

3. Which number does point C best represent on the number line?

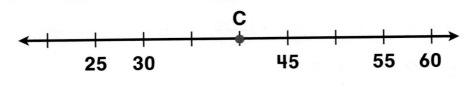

40	32	44	35
○	○	○	○

TEKS 2.8 (page 25)

4. Which letter on the number line best represents 51?

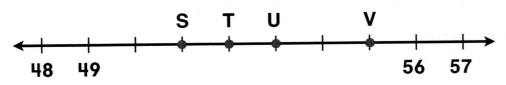

S	T	U	V
○	○	○	○

TEKS 2.8 (page 25)

Education Place
Visit **www.eduplace.com/txmap/** for
Test-Taking Tips and Extra Practice.

308

Spiral Review

Name _____

Greg Tang's Go Fast, Go Far

Add 9

Adding 9 is fast and fun.
First add 10 then take away 1!

I start with
16 + 10 = 26. Since I've
added 1 too many, I
take away 1 from 26
and get 25.

1. 16 + 9 = ☐ **25**

   ☐ **10** – ☐ **1**

2. 37 + 9 = ☐

   ☐ – ☐

3. 45 + 9 = ☐

   ☐ – ☐

Keep It Up!

4. 18 + 9 = ☐

   ☐ ☐

5. 23 + 9 = ☐

   ☐ ☐

Take It Further: Now try all the steps in
your head!

6. 79 + 9 = ☐

7. 86 + 9 = ☐

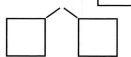
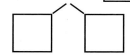

Name _____

Reading and Writing Math

There are three hundred sixty-five days in one year. One way to show that number is in a **place-value chart**.

Hundreds	Tens	Ones
3	6	5

Word Bank
addition
digit
hundreds
place-value
 chart

Complete the word web for the number 365.

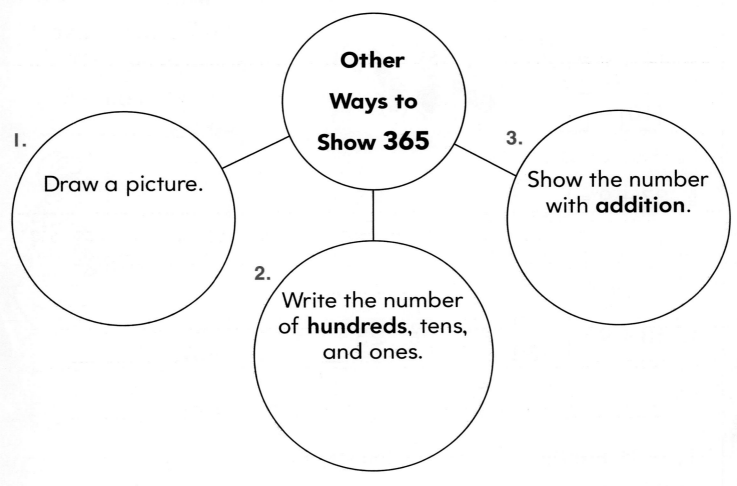

Other Ways to Show 365

1. Draw a picture.

2. Write the number of **hundreds**, tens, and ones.

3. Show the number with **addition**.

4. **Writing Math** Find out the number of students in your grade. Make a word web like the one above showing that number.

TEKS 2.13A Explain and record observations using objects, words, pictures, numbers, and technology.   TEKS 2.13B Relate informal language to mathematical language and symbols.

Name _____

Concepts and Skills

Write the number. TEKS 2.1A, 2.1B

1. 4 █ ,
   6 ▭▭ , and 5 ▪.

Hundreds	Tens	Ones

_____

2. 3 █ ,
   1 ▭▭ , and 4 ▪.

Hundreds	Tens	Ones

_____

3. 900 + 50 + 6 _____

4. 1 + 70 + 100 _____

5. 600 + 40 + 5 _____

Write the number. TEKS 2.1C

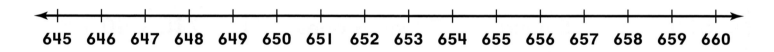

645 646 647 648 649 650 651 652 653 654 655 656 657 658 659 660

Before	Between	After
6. _____, 653	654, _____, 656	657, _____
7. _____, 660	645, _____, 647	648, _____

Compare the numbers. TEKS 2.1C

Write >, <, or = in the ◯.

8. 463 ◯ 471

9. 828 ◯ 828

10. 326 ◯ 236

Write the numbers in order from greatest to least. TEKS 2.1B, 2.1C

11. 109   110   106   100   _____ _____ _____ _____

12. 345   315   430   451   _____ _____ _____ _____

13. 890   980   950   850   _____ _____ _____ _____

14. 246   256   360   240   _____ _____ _____ _____

15. 200   230   302   203   _____ _____ _____ _____

Circle another way to show the number. TEKS 2.1A, 2.1B

16. 862	6 hundreds 8 tens 2 ones	800 + 60 + 2
17. 326	☐☐☐‖ ₀₀₀₀₀	200 + 30 + 6
18. 574	5 hundreds 7 tens 4 ones	700 + 40 + 5
19. 132	100 + 20 + 3	

Problem Solving

Complete the table to solve. TEKS 2.6A, 2.12C

20. The concert hall sells 100 tickets each day.
How many tickets do they sell in 5 days?

Day	1				
Tickets	100				

_____ tickets

Copyright © Houghton Mifflin Company. All rights reserved.